Above: Saint Jerome, writing in his study. Engraving by Albrecht Dürer, 1514.

First published 2019
This edition © Amy Jones 2024
Cartoon copyrights © *shown on page iv*

Published by Wooden Books Ltd.
Glastonbury, Somerset

British Library Cataloguing in Publication Data
Jones, A.
Literary Devices

A CIP catalogue record for this book
may be obtained from the British Library

ISBN-10: 1-904263-06-2
ISBN-13: 978-1-904263-06-7

All rights reserved.
For permission to reproduce any part of this
literary treasure please contact the publishers.

Designed and typeset in Glastonbury, UK.

Printed in India on FSC® certified papers by
Quarterfold Printabilities Pvt. Ltd.

LITERARY DEVICES

Amy Jones

Special thanks to Aubrey, Emma and Farés—three very different sources of inspiration and motivation in the writing of this little book.

Recommended further reading: Percy Lubbock, *The Craft of Fiction*; Aristotle, *Poetics*; George Orwell, *Why I Write*; Northrop Frye, *Anatomy of Criticism*; Alberto Manguel, *A History of Reading*; David Crystal, *The Little Book of Language*; Stephen King, *On Writing: the Memoir of a Craft*; Margaret Atwood, *On Writers and Writing*; Ursula Le Guin, *Steering the Craft*; Dorothea Brande, *Becoming a Writer*; *The Writers' and Artists' Yearbook*.

All cartoons remain © original copyright holders and may not be reproduced. They are licenced for this book via www.Cartoonstock.com (*pages 9, 18, 23, 27, 28, 33, 34, 37, 39, 41, 45, 46 & 53*), Chainsawsuit.com (*pages 5 & 56*), Zits Partnership distributed by King Features via All Sorts Media (*pages 12 & 57*), Andertoons.com (*page 15*), Bizarrocomics.com (*page 21 & 49*), Glenn Mccoy (*page 29*), xkcd.com (*page 31*) and Invisibules.org (*page 55*).

Introduction	1
Lost in a Book	2
Rules of Thumb	
Show Don't Tell!	4
Keep it Simple Stupid!	6
Blow it Up!	8
Read it Aloud!	10
Figurative Language	12
Emphasis & Understatement	
Hyperbole	14
Meiosis & Litotes	16
Accumulation & Amplification	18
Anaphora & Epiphora	20
Antithesis & Juxtaposition	22
Oxymoron & Paralipsis	24
Resemblance & Relationship	
Anthropomorphism	26
Personification & Zoomorphism	28
Metaphor	30
Simile & Analogy	32
Synecdoche & Metonymy	34
Motif	36
Trope	38
Verbal Games	
Adnomination & Paronomasia	40
Anastrophe, Antimetabole & Chiasmus	42
Kenning & Portmanteau	44
Paradox, Bathos & Paraprosdokian	46
Tmesis, Spoonerism & Zeugma	48
Figures of Sound	
Cacophony, Euphony & Onomatopoeia	50
Alliteration, Assonance & Consonance	52
Errors	
Malapropism & Mondegreen	54
Tautology & Reduplication	56
Rules for Writers	58

Wood engraving by Gustave Doré for the 1877 illustrated edition of the 1798 poem The Rime of the Ancient Mariner by Samuel Taylor Coleridge.

INTRODUCTION

WHAT IS THE WRITER'S CRAFT? How is it done? A good writer can create a story that is so compelling and convincing that readers become completely absorbed in the characters and narratives spun around them. The reader forgets that hobbits are not real and begins to believe that mystical kingdoms exist inside wardrobes. This effect was famously described by Samuel Taylor Coleridge as the 'willing suspension of disbelief'. Coleridge writes of a conversation he had with his friend, poet William Wordsworth, where they discussed the line that authors walk, between the

> *... two cardinal points of poetry, the power of exciting the sympathy of the reader by a faithful adherence to the truth of nature, and the power of giving the interest of novelty by the modifying colours of imagination.* S. T. Coleridge, Biographia Literaria

Over two millennia earlier, the Greek philosophers Plato and Aristotle had considered similar themes. Plato dismissed artistic representations as poor copies of divine forms and of reality. Aristotle, however, responded that all human beings had an urge to imitate nature and the world around them and that it was a good thing that art and literature were moderately removed from reality (while convincingly similar), as it allowed the audience (or reader) to safely undergo *catharsis*, a purging of emotions brought about by experiencing something tragic play out on the stage (or page).

In this little book, we will examine some of the tricks of the trade that writers use to arrange words in sentences and paragraphs. Methods and decisions involving longer structures, such as those which apply to plot, story and narrative, are covered in sister books *Plot* and *Narrative Devices*.

So, to find out how authors build whole worlds from words, read on.

Lost in a Book
imagine the sight, the sound, the smell

How do you make a reader suspend their disbelief? While Wordsworth easily conjures a host of golden daffodils, Coleridge asks us to believe that his narrator is the only man alive on a drifting ship full of zombies:

> They groaned, they stirred, they all uprose,
>   Ne spake, ne moved their eyes;
> It had been strange, even in a dream,
>   To have seen those dead men rise. S. T. Coleridge, *The Rime of the Ancient Mariner*

He achieves the effect by beginning his tale in an everyday setting (outside a church at the beginning of a wedding), and by using an unreliable narrator (a *grey-beard loon*) relating a tale set in an ambiguous place and time.

Research shows that when we read fiction (or watch some news or a movie), we experience different degrees of 'narrative transportation', and this affects the way that we look at the world, sometimes for years after.

Importantly, the three biggest enhancers of such transportations are:

1. **VERISIMILITUDE**, or relatability. A story established in an everyday setting using **MIMESIS**, the activation of the imagination through the mimicking of sights and sounds (and smells, tastes and feelings).

2. **ATTACHMENT** to the protagonist, or as Kurt Vonnegut puts it (*see page 58*) having 'someone to root for'—the reader needs to empathise with the protagonist, even if they are an antihero.

3. **CONFLICT** in the narrative. Conflict creates and captures the reader's interest, as *external* action and dialogue between characters (and their agendas), and as *internal* struggles between their habits and choices.

It is not only the reader who is transported. In Shakespeare's comedies, *Twelfth Night* and *A Midsummer Night's Dream*, the narratives also begin in a recognisable world, before moving to an 'other' world that is removed, and then finally returning to the 'normal' world again. The 'normal' world and the 'other' world are intertwined and inform one another.

This device is particularly useful in genres that require higher degrees of suspension of disbelief, such as Gothic, Fantasy, Sci Fi or Comedy. The openings of Bram Stoker's 1897 *Dracula* and John Wyndham's Sci Fi classic *The Day of the Triffids* use almost tedious descriptions of everyday detail:

> Why the founders of St. Merryn's Hospital chose to erect their institution at a main-road crossing upon a valuable office site, and thus expose their patients' nerves to constant laceration, is a foible that I never properly understood. But for those fortunate enough to be suffering from complaints unaffected by the wear and tear of continuous traffic, it did have the advantage that one could lie abed and still not be out of touch, so to speak, with the flow of life. Customarily the west-bound busses thundered along trying to beat the lights at the corner; as often as not a pig-squeal of brakes and a salvo of shots from the silencer would tell that they hadn't. Then the released cross traffic would rev and roar as it started up the incline. And every now and then there would be an interlude: a good grinding bump, followed by a general stoppage— exceedingly tantalizing to one in my condition ... But this morning was different. John Wyndham *The Day of the Triffids*

By establishing a recognisable norm early in the text, an entire novel may even be based on a spaceship and yet succeed due to VERISIMILITUDE (from the Latin *verum* "truth" and *similis* "similar") in the relationships between the characters. This is delivered through MIMESIS (from the Greek *mimeisthai* "to mimic") in description and dialogue which reflects the evolving situation by mimicking everyday sights and sounds, as in the sensory descriptions of traffic moving outside of a hospital, above. These magical tools allow writers to transport their readers to different worlds.

SHOW DON'T TELL!
the golden rule

The deep-rooted rule of showing-not-telling says that a writer should not spoon-feed ('tell') the reader what is going on but instead ('show') objects and characters interacting with the setting or another character.

Thus, instead of telling a reader:

It was a cold rainy day in November.

a writer might imply the setting:

Seeing the thin grey light of the winter morning, she buttoned her coat tightly against her throat, deftly plucked an umbrella from the stand and splashed out into the cold street.

Here, three senses are triggered: the visual (light and the street), touch (sensation of coat around neck) and sound (splashing). The verbs and adverbs describe the character responding to the environment: the tight buttoning, the deft plucking and the marching out establish the setting and convey a confident character with a clear purpose. Implicature is key—the umbrella and the splashing render it unnecessary to state that it is wet and rainy.

Or look at this example, which uses people's reactions as they pass a house to show us, rather than tell us, that the house is haunted:

Outside a driver whipped his horse into the gallop local people felt necessary when they passed 124. Toni Morrisson, *The Beloved*

Film scripts often display superb examples of Show-Don't-Tell:

3 members of the PINHEADS rock band, KEYBOARDS, BASS and DRUMS, exchange nervous glances, repeatedly checking their watches. They're all set up on stage. Robert Zemeckis & Bob Gale, *Back to the Future*

The central motif of time is established in this scene from the opening of the film. We can see that the band are on edge and that their final member is late, rather than wasting dialogue on a clumsy exchange telling us so.

Inexperienced writers often underestimate the imaginative capabilities of their readers, providing them with unrewarding descriptions. Showing-not-telling enhances verisimilitude (*see page 3*), as the reader becomes engaged with the text and immersed in the other world it conjures.

> [T]he novelist ... has ... to render and not to tell. (If I say, "The wicked Mr. Blank shot nice Blanche's dear cat!" that is telling. If I say: "Blank raised his rifle and aimed it at the quivering, black-burdened topmost bough of the cherry-tree. After the report a spattered bunch of scarlet and black quiverings dropped from branch to branch to pancake itself on the orchard grass!" that is rather bad rendering, but still rendering ...). Ford Madox Ford, *The English Novel*

Modern rendering software turns data into visual images; writers render sensory data into creative output. The table below suggests various ways of showing-rather-than-telling a character's frame of mind:

HAPPY	UNHAPPY
giggled and started to laugh	looked at her mascara-streaked cheeks
hug-nuzzled her warmly	clenched his jaw and gripped the table
grinned from ear to ear	put her hands on her hips and glared
jumped up and down and spun around	bit his tongue and held back tears
nodded and clapped energetically	stomped her feet and slammed the door
a huge smile spread across his face	paced around the room like a wolf
danced around the room	frowned and spat at the floor
whistled and then burst into song	veins were popping out
eyes twinkled with amusement	raised his voice and started yelling
punched the air and gave him a high five	hot tears started welling up

KEEP IT SIMPLE STUPID!
less is more

In the 19th century, authors often used elaborate multi-page descriptions of characters, settings or emotions:

> *There had risen before her the girl's vision of a possible future for herself to which she looked forward with trembling hope, and she wanted to wander on in that visionary future without interruption. She walked briskly in the brisk air, the colour rose in her cheeks, and her straw-bonnet (which our contemporaries might look at with conjectural curiosity as at an obsolete form of basket) fell a little backward. She would perhaps be hardly characterised enough if it were omitted that she wore her brown hair flatly braided and coiled behind so as to expose the outline of her head in a daring manner at a time when public feeling required the meagreness of nature to be dissimulated by tall barricades of frizzed curls and bows, never surpassed by any great race except the Feejeean.* George Eliot *Middlemarch*

Today, readers and critics have largely lost patience with such prose. In an age that values economy in communication, best practice is generally to avoid ornate description and instead 'Keep It Simple Stupid' or K.I.S.S. SIMPLICITY involves CONCISION and CLARITY, and often results in BREVITY:

> **Brevity is the sole of wit** wordy Polonius in Shakespeare's *Hamlet*

Rumour has it that Ernest Hemingway once bet that he could write an entire story in just six words (a forerunner of Twitter and flash fiction):

> **For sale: baby shoes, never worn.** Ernest Hemingway

Short stories are an an excellent way of practicing K.I.S.S. The short story form demands concision and economy. In many ways, it is far more demanding than the longer novel. Roald Dahl agrees:

> *Study Hemingway, particularly his early work and learn how to write short sentences and how to eschew all those beastly adjectives. Surely it is better to say "She was a tall girl with a bosom" than "She was a tall girl with a shapely, prominent bosom", or some such rubbish. The first one says it all.* Roald Dahl Letter to Jay Williams

Chekov was another master of the short story. One of his notebooks contains this condensed sketch:

> A man in Monte Carlo goes to the casino, wins a million, returns home, commits suicide.

Film scripts convey description with great efficiency, leaving it to the reader or director to visualise most of the content except the dialogue:

> MOTHER (To the doctor): He's been depressed. All off a sudden, he can't do anything.
> DOCTOR (Nodding): Why are you depressed, Alvy?
> MOTHER: (Nudging Alvy) Tell Dr. Flicker.
> (Young Alvy sits, his head down. His mother answers for him) It's something he read.
> DOCTOR (Puffing on his cigarette and nodding) Something he read, huh?
> ALVY: (His head still down) The universe is expanding.
> DOCTOR: The universe is expanding? Woody Allen, Annie Hall

Concision is everywhere today. Every writer and scriptwriter is taught to cut excess adjectives and adverbs, overlong passages, sentences and words, and weak dialogue, metaphors and anecdotes. Every marketeer and entrepreneur learns how to craft, hone and perfect the 1-minute 'elevator pitch'.

BLOW IT UP!
zooming in

Although economy is king in modern writing, there will always be the occasional passage where detail is both effective and necessary. Part of the author's craft lies in recognising this and BLOWING UP these special moments by indulging in a well-placed descriptive passage—for good reason.

Take for example *The Odyssey*. This epic poem covers great swathes of time and place in its course, but Homer spends time 'blowing up' a small scar on his hero's thigh—a significant plot device as it is recognised by a former retainer from an injury that Odysseus sustained in his youth and is then used as a springboard for a flashback detailing the event.

In another example (*below*), Conan Doyle needs to capture the mood of the moors where his mystery is set:

> The wagonette swung round into a side road, and we curved upward through deep lanes worn by centuries of wheels, high banks on either side, heavy with dripping moss and fleshy hart's-tongue ferns. Bronzing bracken and mottled bramble gleamed in the light of the sinking sun. Still steadily rising, we passed over a narrow granite bridge, and skirted a noisy stream which gushed swiftly down, foaming and roaring amid the grey boulders. Both road and stream wound up through a valley dense with scrub oak and fir... Yellow leaves carpeted the lanes and fluttered down upon us as we passed. Arthur Conan Doyle, The Hound of the Baskervilles

He goes on to set up a tone of isolation, a stark contrast from the city in which we meet our principal characters, an example of using verisimilitude to encourage a willing suspension of disbelief (*see pages 1–3*). By removing the characters to a foreign and unwelcoming landscape, we are more likely to buy into the potential reality of the mysterious events that follow.

An author should be able to identify characters, settings or motifs (*see page 36*) that are significant either to the narrative or to establishing mood. For example, in Proust's 'madeleine moment', the simple act of consuming a cake transports our narrator into his remembrances:

> [O]ne day in winter, on my return home, my mother, seeing that I was cold, offered me some tea, a thing I did not ordinarily take. I declined at first, and then, for no particular reason, changed my mind. She sent for one of those squat, plump little cakes called 'petites madeleines', which look as though they had been moulded in the fluted valve of a scallop shell. And soon, mechanically, dispirited after a dreary day with the prospect of a depressing morrow, I raised to my lips a spoonful of the tea in which I had soaked a morsel of the cake. No sooner had the warm liquid mixed with the crumbs touched my palate than a shiver ran through me and I stopped, intent upon the extraordinary thing that was happening to me. An exquisite pleasure had invaded my senses, something isolated, detached, with no suggestion of its origin. Marcel Proust, In Search of Lost Time, Vol 1: Swann's Way

"Your curriculum vitae is extremely detailed, isn't it? I don't quite know what to make of the fact that your third-grade teacher, Miss Hartley, made you stand in the corner for throwing an eraser although another kid did it."

READ IT ALOUD!
the art of euphonics

The *sound* of words, sentences and paragraphs is highly important. Writers often advise reading aloud as an aid to identify unintentionally clumsy passages and subtle bumps in cadence—the rhythm and pulse of a piece can have as much impact on meaning as the words themselves:

> You start realizing that good prose is crunchy. There's texture in your mouth as you say it. You realize bad writing, bland writing, has no texture, no taste, no corners in your mouth. I'm a great believer in reading aloud. Janet Fitch, author of White Oleander

> I don't find writing easy. That is because I do take great care: I rewrite a lot. If anything is sort of clumsy and not possible to read aloud to oneself, which I think one should do ... it doesn't work. Ruth Rendell, crime writer

> Hear me now or regret it later: Everything you write must be read aloud... you have been listening to the English language at least five or six years longer than you have been writing and reading ... your ears know when things sound okay, good, beautiful strange, awkward, or just plain bad, before your eye can pick up on such things. Jiro Adachi, author of The Island of Bicycle Dancers

Individual sounds have specific qualities. Plato's treatise on the naming of things, *Cratylus*, discusses the difference between words with soft consonants such as *m*, *n* and *l* and those with hard consonants such as *k* and *g*. Linguists professor David Crystal asks us to imagine an alien planet with two races, the *Lamonians* and the *Grataks*. Which sounds friendlier?

When choosing a new name, male actors tend to avoid soft *m* sounds and favour harder consonants, e.g. *Marion Michael Morrison* became *John Wayne* and *Mark Sinclair* became *Vin Diesel*. Female actors go the other way: *Norma Jean Baker* became *Marilyn Monroe* and *Helen Hackford* became *Helen Mirren*.

The principle can be employed to name fictional creatures and characters. Dickens is a master at this: consider the unpleasant *Uriah Heep* from *David Copperfield* with his abrupt *p* ending and creeping *ee* sound, a sharp contrast to the soft sound of beautiful and naïve *Dora Spenlow*.

Similarly, in descriptions, the sounds of key words create a tonal effect. A seaside scene might have a *low gentle lapping of ocean* (the gentle *sh* of *ocean* and alliterated lateral *l*-sound painting a relaxed picture) or *a chorus of crashing waves* (its harsh *c* and *v* portraying a tumultuous sea). Here is a list:

LONG VOWEL SOUNDS: *aah, eee, iye, owe, ooo* + SOFT CONSONANTS *m, l, n, t* = pleasant melodious sounds: *Let's meet on the moor by the light of the moon my love.*

SHORT VOWEL SOUNDS: *a, eh, ih, oh, uh* + HARD CONSONANTS *p, b, k, d, t* = harsh, dramatic sounds: *The pike bit down hard.*

SIBILANTS: *s, z, j, ch, sc, sh, st* + short vowels + hard consonants = a sinister or unsettled feeling, *The skeleton snapped his jaw*, or + long vowels + soft consonants can create a soothing, lulling tone: *Sweet sleep with soft down.*

FRICATIVES: *f, v, th* involve placing the tongue between the teeth. Their frivolous quality can be heard in *Fancy a fling, you vampy old fart?*

PLOSIVES: *b, p, d, t, g, c, k, q* require the speaker to 'explode' air from the mouth, creating outbursts: *Get your stinking paws off me, you damned dirty ape.*

NASALS: *m, n* (as we have seen) are soft homely sounds: *Mummy, I miss nanny.*

LATERALS: *l* creates a gentle, harmonious tone: *Dally in lovely long languid lanes.*

TRILLS & FLAPS: *r, gg, tt, dd* create a rough texture: *Gutted with a ragged dagger.*

DIPHTHONGS & TRIPTHONGS: *aye, oi, igh, ow, ur* require us to change our mouth shape as we say them. They slow down text, making it sound more ponderous: *The boy coiled his mouth like a lure* or *I wandered lonely as a cloud.*

FIGURATIVE LANGUAGE
words drawing pictures

'Figurative' (from the Latin *figura*, 'to form or fashion') is a blanket term used to describe any non-literal language. Whereas LITERAL LANGUAGE conveys *fact*, FIGURATIVE LANGUAGE conveys *meaning* in an abstract or emotive way, the embellished writing painting a picture for the reader:

> I was as hollow and empty as the spaces between the stars. R. Chandler, *The Long Goodbye*

Readers enjoy the relatability of a shared experience pinned down in an innovative way. George Orwell's first rule of writing was *Never use a metaphor, simile or other figure of speech which you are used to seeing in print*.

Although every writer uses figurative language, not every sentence needs to bubble over with clever literary devices—many a good plot is lost in overly florid language. Flaubert was particularly aware of his weakness for metaphors, referring to them as 'vermin'. In *Madame Bovary* his occasional flourishes are all the more impactful for their rarity, such as this graphic example from the funeral of his eponymous protagonist:

> They had to lift her head a little and at that a stream of black liquid ran out of her mouth like vomit. Gustave Flaubert, *Madame Bovary*

Figurative language is also an excellent tool for *characterisation*, particularly when using *first person narrative perspective* to describe a character's nature or appearance:

> Nearly everyone preferred Aron with his golden hair and the openness that allowed his affection to plunge like a puppy. John Steinbeck, East of Eden

Figurative language can also appear within a character's *narrative voice* to tell us something more subtle about their nature. In his overly chivalric use of language Cervantes perfectly encapsulates Don Quixote's noble but comically misguided nature when proclaiming his love for Dulcinea:

> Were it not for the might that she infuses into my arm I should not have strength enough to kill a flea. Miguel de Cervantes, Don Quixote

Similarly, Jane Austen in *Northanger Abbey* personifies the storm that surrounds Catherine Morland as she explores the Gothic mansion at night:

> Catherine, as she crossed the hall, listened to the tempest with sensations of awe; and, when she heard it rage round a corner of the ancient building and close with sudden fury a distant door, felt for the first time that she was really in an abbey.

Figurative language has five different forms:

1. **Emphasis & Understatement** – e.g. placing contrasting words next to one another to highlight the extremity of emotion (*pages 14–25*).
2. **Relationship & Resemblance** – establishing comparisons or links between subjects (*pages 26–39*).
3. **Verbal Games** – wit and wordplay (*pages 40–49*).
4. **Figures of Sound** – using phonetics to impact the meaning conveyed (*pages 50–53*).
5. **Errors** – language misused for comedic effect (*pages 54–57*).

Hyperbole
totally over the top

HYPERBOLE is a common figurative device, the deliberate use of overexaggeration for effect: *I nearly died of embarrassment; You've been told a million times; They've got tons of money; Darling, that was the best.* Aristotle refers to users of hyperbolic language as juvenile, but Quintilian, in his *Institutes of Oratory* (c. 95 AD), takes a more forgiving approach:

> *In a word, the hyperbole is a beauty, when the thing itself, of which we have to speak, is in its nature extraordinary; for we are then allowed to say a little more than the truth, because the exact truth cannot be said; and language is more efficient when it goes beyond reality than when it stops short of it.*

Hyperbole can create a variety of effects. Here's a famous example of comedic overexaggeration written by the Monty Python team:

> MICHAEL PALIN: *You were lucky! We lived for three months in a brown paper bag in a septic tank. We used to have to get up at six o'clock in the morning, clean the bag, eat a crust of stale bread, go to work down mill for 14 hours a day week in, week out. When we got home, our Dad would thrash us to sleep with his belt!*
>
> GRAHAM CHAPMAN: *Luxury! We used to have to get out of the lake at three o'clock in the morning, clean the lake, eat a handful of hot gravel, go to work at the mill every day for tuppence a month, come home, and Dad would beat us around the head and neck with a broken bottle, if we were lucky!*
>
> TERRY GILLIAM: *Well we had it tough. We used to have to get up out of the shoebox at 12 o'clock at night and lick the road clean with our tongues. We had half a handful of freezing cold gravel, worked 24 hours a day at the mill for fourpence every six years, and when we got home, our Dad would slice us in two with a bread knife.*

> ERIC IDLE: *I had to get up in the morning at 10 o'clock at night, half an hour before I went to bed, eat a lump of cold poison, work 29 hours a day down mill, and pay mill owner for permission to come to work, and when we got home, our Dad would kill us, and dance about on our graves singing 'Hallelujah'.* At Last the 1948 Show, Four Yorkshiremen

Hyperbole can also be used to capture a particular spoken register:

> *Well now, one winter it was so cold that all the geese flew backward and all the fish moved south and even the snow turned blue. Late at night, it got so frigid that all spoken words froze solid afore they could be heard. People had to wait until sunup to find out what folks were talking about the night before.* S.E. Schlosser Babe the Blue Ox

Gabriel García Márquez, a founder of the Magical Realism movement, uses it to uncanny effect in his autobiography, *Living to Tell the Tale*:

> *At that time Bogotá was a remote, lugubrious city where an insomniac rain had been falling since the beginning of the sixteenth century.* G. G. Marquez Living to Tell the Tale

Hyperbole can also be used in characterisation; a hyperbolic character tends to be one who is melodramatic and not entirely likeable. Here is Tennessee Williams' Blanche Dubois from *A Streetcar Named Desire*:

> *I don't want realism ... I'll tell you what I want. Magic! ... Yes, yes, magic! I try to give that to people. I misrepresent things to them. I don't tell the truth, I tell what ought to be the truth. And if that is sinful, then let me be damned for it!* T. Williams, A Streetcar Named Desire

Steve Jobs gets ready for his keynote.

MEIOSIS & LITOTES
it's nothing really, not unusual

MEIOSIS and its sibling, LITOTES, are both antonyms for hyperbole. Instead of ramping it up and laying it on thick, litotes and meiosis instead involve the more subtle arts of deliberate underexaggeration and ironic understatement.

Meiosis, from the Greek *meioo* 'to make smaller', involves downplaying the significance of something—often unpleasant. The Northern Irish civil war becomes The Troubles, Mercutio's mortal wound in Shakespeare's *Romeo and Juliet* becomes "A scratch, a scratch". Roald Dahl frequently utilises meiosis to great comedic effect, as in this extract from his autobiography:

> So they simply amputated the arm at the elbow, and for the rest of his life my father had to manage with one arm ... The loss of an arm, he used to say, caused him only one serious inconvenience. He found it impossible to cut the top off a boiled egg. R. Dahl, *Boy*

Continuing the medical theme, here is another example:

> "It's really an awfully simple operation, Jig," the man said. "It's not really an operation at all."
> The girl looked at the ground the table legs rested on.
> "I know you wouldn't mind it, Jig. It's really not anything. It's just to let the air in." Ernest Hemingway, *Hills Like White Elephants*

LITOTES differs from meiosis in that it downplays what is being said by negating its opposite. Thus we commonly hear: Not bad at all; You won't regret it; She's hardly the brightest button in the box; It's not wrong to say that; This is no minor matter. Litotes often take the form 'X is not un-Y', where Y is what is basically intended. Double negatives are used to soften, spice or undermine a strong opinion, or to disguise something nice or nasty.

Litotes is an ancient device. In *The Iliad*, Zeus describes Achilles as:

> οὔτε γάρ ἔστ᾽ ἄφρων οὔτ᾽ ἄσκοπος — neither unthinking, nor unseeing."

Here is F. Scott Fitzgerald's narrator, Nick Carraway, describing the neighborhoods of East Egg and West Egg in *The Great Gatsby*:

> I lived at West Egg, the — well, the less fashionable of the two, though this is a most superficial tag to express the bizarre and not a little sinister contrast between them.

And here is a circumspect way of describing a man:

> Not improbably, it was to this latter class of men that Mr. Dimmesdale, by many of his traits of character, naturally belonged.   Nathaniel Hawthorne *The Scarlet Letter*

When Samuel Johnson tells us that *to write is, indeed, no unpleasing employment*, there is an air of nonchalance, almost a very English sangfroid, in the understatement. Indeed, in many examples of these figures, the cool downplaying and inversion of the thing serves to make a feature of its bashful unassumingness, and so it becomes even more interesting.

Not all readers and critics appreciate the use of litotes, however. George Orwell describes his particular distate for it in *Why I Write*:

> One can cure oneself of the not un- formation by memorizing this sentence:
> A not unblack dog was chasing a not unsmall rabbit across a not ungreen field.

ACCUMULATION & AMPLIFICATION
good, true and beautiful

ACCUMULATION (Latin *accumulationem* 'a heaping up') involves building a group of words or phrases which conveys passion and frustration:

> PRINCE HENRY: A tun of man is thy companion. Why dost thou converse with that trunk of humors, that bolting-hutch of beastliness, that swollen parcel of dropsies, that huge bombard of sack, that stuffed cloakbag of guts, that roasted Manningtree ox with the pudding in his belly, that reverend Vice, that gray iniquity, that father ruffian, that vanity in years? William Shakespeare, Henry IV Part I

In a modern example from the movie *Gladiator*, the protagonist lists the wrongs that have befallen to him, thus legitimising his desire for revenge:

> My name is Maximus Decimus Meridius, Commander of the Armies of the North, General of the Felix Legions, loyal servant to the true emperor, Marcus Aurelius. Father to a murdered son, husband to a murdered wife. And I will have my vengeance, in this life or the next.
>
> Screenplay David Franzoni (rev. John Logan)

A famous example of accumulation, used to emphasise the fatalistic quality of the encounter, occurs in Michael Curtiz's 1942 movie *Casablanca*:

> Of all the gin joints in all the towns in all the world, she walks into mine.
>
> J. J. Epstein

AMPLIFICATION emphasises and draws attention to a significant word, phrase, trope or motif using repetition and expansion:

> This is a crisis. A large crisis. In fact … it's a twelve-story crisis with a magnificent entrance hall, carpeting throughout, 24-hour portage, and an enormous sign on the roof, saying THIS IS A LARGE CRISIS. Richard Curtis & Ben Elton, Blackadder Goes Forth

Amplification has many uses. Brendan McGuigan, author of *Rhetorical Devices: A Handbook and Activities for Student Writers* suggests:

> The main purpose of amplification is to focus the reader's attention on an idea he or she might otherwise miss.

Margaret Atwood amplifies small details or emotions at key moments in a narrative to encapsulate a character's appearance or frame of mind, as in the following extract from *The Handmaid's Tale*:

> What I need is perspective. The illusion of depth, created by a frame, the arrangement of shapes on a flat surface. Perspective is necessary. Otherwise there are only two dimensions. Otherwise you live with your face squashed up against a wall, everything a huge foreground, of details, close-ups, hairs, the weave of the bedsheet, the molecules of the face. Your own skin like a map, a diagram of futility, crisscrossed with tiny roads that lead nowhere. Otherwise you live in the moment. Which is not where I want to be.

Amplification is a common feature of children's writing where it can add a sense of fun, rhythm and drama, and help expand young vocabularies. Repeated nouns are often modified with changing adjectives, as in the much-loved *We're Going on a Bear Hunt* by Michael Rosen:

> Uh-uh! A forest!   A big dark forest.
> Uh-uh! A snowstorm!   A swirling whirling snowstorm.
> Uh-uh! A cave!   A narrow gloomy cave.

Anaphora & Epiphora
repetition repetition

ANAPHORA and EPIPHORA use repetition to create emphasis. ANAPHORA is the repetition of the same phase or word at the *beginning* of nearby clauses or sentences: *Right you! Get over! Right here! Right now!* EPIPHORA, by contrast, repeats the word or phrase at the *end* of nearby clauses or sentences: *You're wrong! He's wrong! She's wrong!* Both are intrinsically rhythmic. Both were widely used in the ancient world, as this Old Testament anaphora shows:

> *I have come into my garden, my sister, my bride.*
> *I have gathered my myrrh with my spice;*
> *I have eaten my honeycomb with my honey;*
> *I have drunk my wine with my milk.* Song of Songs

English Renaissance authors rediscovered anaphora in new translations of the Bible; Shakespeare uses it in the opening lines of *Macbeth* to build a sense of impending unease via the shared repetition of 'when':

> FIRST WITCH: *When shall we three meet again?*
> *In thunder, lightning, or in rain?*
> SECOND WITCH: *When the hurly-burly's done,*
> ***When the battle's lost and won.*** William Shakespeare, *Macbeth*

Within a paragraph, structures created by anaphora can be used to amplify the subject and subtly build metaphor (*see page 30*):

> *Summer was on the way; Jem and I awaited it with impatience. Summer was our best season: it was sleeping on the back screened porch in cots, or trying to sleep in the treehouse; summer was everything good to eat; it was a thousand colors in a parched landscape; but most of all, summer was Dill.* Harper Lee, To Kill a Mockingbird

Anaphora is a common feature of film and television writing, where it is used to create climax and emphasis through accumulation (*see page 18*), as in this line from Elia Kazan's 1954 movie *On the Waterfront*:

> *You don't understand. I coulda had class. I coulda been a contender. I coulda been somebody, instead of a bum, which is what I am, let's face it.* Budd Schulberg

With repeated words or phrases at the end instead of the start of clauses, EPIPHORA (also known as EPISTROPHE) can strongly focus attention on a particular theme or idea. Here is another example from the Bible:

> *When I was a child, I spake as a child, I understood as a child, I thought as a child: but when I became a man, I put away childish things.* Corinthians

The child of anaphora and epistrophe is SYMPLOCE, which has repetitions at the beginnings *and* endings, e.g. *You want the truth? You can't handle the truth!*:

> *Then I'll be all aroun' in the dark. I'll be ever'where — wherever you look. Wherever they's a fight so hungry people can eat, I'll be there. Wherever they's a cop beatin' up a guy, I'll be there ... An' when our folk eat the stuff they raise an' live in the houses they build — why, I'll be there.*
>
> John Steinbeck, *The Grapes of Wrath*

Remember, although words may repeat, they can have very different meanings in different contexts (*left, and see too page 57*).

ANTITHESIS & JUXTAPOSITION
for richer or poorer

ANTITHESIS (Greek *anti* 'against' + *tithenai* 'to put, place') places two things in opposition to create a balanced contrast. It can create a sense of tension and conflict but also be wielded for its emphasis and sagacity:

> To err is human; to forgive divine. Alexander Pope, An Essay on Criticism
>
> Love is an ideal thing, marriage a real thing. Johann W von Goethe, Letter to Friedrich von Müller
>
> Give every man thy ear, but few thy voice. William Shakespeare, Hamlet
>
> I would rather be ashes than dust! | I would rather that my spark should burn out | in a brilliant blaze than it should be stifled by dryrot. | I would rather be a superb meteor, every atom | of me in magnificent glow, than a sleepy and permanent planet. | The proper function of man is to live, not to exist. | I shall not waste my days in trying to prolong them. | I shall use my time. Jack London

Antithesis also occurs between characters. Antithetical characters can be opposite in various ways: e.g. rich–poor, young–old, good–evil:

> Snow White <—> jealous queen   Cinderella <—> wicked stepmother
> Harry Potter <—> Lord Voldemort   Luke Skywalker <—> Darth Vader

In Salman Rushdie's *The Satanic Verses*, the character Farishta takes on the personality of the archangel Gabriel, and Chamcha that of a devil.

Antithesis also occurs in argumentative dialogue:

> HUNTER: This gun is loaded!
> BUGS BUNNY: You're lying!
> HUNTER: Wrong again!

Note how each phrase is the antithesis of the preceding one.

JUXTAPOSITION is weaker than antithesis. It places two things in parallel to draw contrasts and comparisons. All figurative devices create images in the reader's mind, and juxtaposition uses two to create emphasis:

> *My mistress' eyes are nothing like the sun;*
> *Coral is far more red than her lips' red;*
> *If snow be white, why then her breasts are dun;*
> *If hairs be wires, black wires grow on her head.*
> *I have seen roses damask'd, red and white,*
> *But no such roses see I in her cheeks;*
> *And in some perfumes is there more delight*
> *Than in the breath that from my mistress reeks.* William Shakespeare, Sonnet 130

Shakespeare juxtaposes clichéd naturalistic images of beauty ('false compare') with the honest reality of his mistress's appearance. In another example, Victor Hugo uses juxtaposition to show-not-tell the transient and impermanent existence of humans in comparison to nature:

> *There were corpses here and there and pools of blood. I remember seeing a butterfly flutter up and down that street. Summer does not abdicate.* Victor Hugo, Les Misérables

Unexpected juxtaposition creates IRONY, one of the core comedic devices, along with *Repetition (pp.21-21, inc. broken repetition)*, *Hyperbole (p.14)*, *Litotes (p.17)*, *Double Entendre, Punning & Verbal Games (pp.40-49)*, *Mistaken Identity (e.g. p.54)*, *Taboo, Timing* and *Slapstick*.

"Next song's called Dirt-poor Boxcar Man which I wrote partly in the VIP lounge at JFK and partly in my private limo on the way here tonight."

OXYMORON
clearly confused

An OXYMORON is a phrase which contains two words that contradict each other or have opposite meanings (ANTONYMS). It is figurative in that what is described is semantically impossible: *I feel like the living dead*; *It was the only choice*; *It's an open secret*; *There was a deafening silence* (note these oxymorons consist of an adjective that opposes the noun). Writers use oxymorons to represent a conflict, contradiction or state of high emotional flux:

> ... *the man trampled calmly over the child's body*   R L Stephenson, Dr Jekyll and Mr Hyde

> *She held herself tight to him and her lips looked for his and then found them and were against them and he felt her, fresh, new and smooth and young and lovely with the warm, scalding coolness and unbelievable to be there.*   Ernest Hemingway, For Whom the Bell Tolls

Shakespeare's *Romeo and Juliet* is full of oxymoronic sentiment as his protagonists struggle between their love for one another and the hatred between their families. Here is Juliet's desperate reaction to the news that her cousin has been murdered by her lover:

> *O serpent heart, hid with a flowering face!*
> *Did ever dragon keep so fair a cave?*
> *Beautiful tyrant! fiend angelical!*
> *Dove-feather'd raven! wolvish-ravening lamb!*   William Shakespeare, Romeo and Juliet

Linguist Richard Lederer has highlighted the modern penchant for oxymoronic phrases, noting the contradictory comedy behind phrases such as *industrial park*, *jumbo shrimp*, *random order*, *peace offensive*, *civil war*, *military intelligence* and *friendly fire*. Of course, George Orwell saw this all coming:

> *War is Peace, Freedom is Slavery, and Ignorance is Strength.*   George Orwell, 1984

PARALIPSIS
not worth comment

PARALIPSIS creates emphasis by omission, i.e. by deliberately not talking about it. This device relies, as does all good writing, on the reader's ability to read between the lines and infer meaning for themselves. John Smith's 1657 *Mysterie of Rhetorique Unvail'd* describes it *as a kind of irony, whereby we deny that we say or doe that which we especially say or doe.* The technique is used very effectively by some of the most famous first person narrators in literature:

> We will not speak of all Queequeg's peculiarities here; how he eschewed coffee and hot rolls, and applied his undivided attention to beefsteaks, done rare. Henry Melville, Moby-Dick

Ishmael, our narrator, emphasises the oddness of Queequeg's foreign habits by alluding to one or two and leaving the rest up to the imagination.

> If you really want to hear about it, the first thing you'll probably want to know is where I was born, and what my lousy childhood was like, and how my parents were occupied and all before they had me, and all that David Copperfield kind of crap, but I don't feel like going into it, if you want to know the truth. J. D. Salinger, The Catcher in the Rye

Salinger's opening lines deliberately buck the traditional novel discourse structure of opening with a brief biography of the narrator in the style of predecessors such as Dickens ('crap'), an aggressive use of metafiction which captures the adolescent defiance of Holden Caulfield. Another example:

> 'Ssh,' said Grace Makutsi, putting a finger to her lips. 'It's not polite to talk about it. So I won't mention the Double Comfort Furniture Shop, which is one of the businesses my fiancé owns, you know. I must not talk about that. But do you know the store, Mma? If you save up, you should come in some day and buy a chair.' Alexander McCall Smith, Blue Shoes and Happiness

ANTHROPOMORPHISM
it seems so human

ANTHROPOMORPHISM is the device of giving human attributes to non-human things. Children's films and books are full of anthropomorphised animals (*Aesop's Fables*, *The Lion King*), toys (*Toy Story*) and vehicles (*Thomas the Tank Engine*, *Cars*). Many modern memes rely on anthropomorphic comedy, for example, a cat that looks like Winston Churchill or a house that looks sad.

Literature and religion have a long tradition of anthropomorphism, with the two being intertwined in many early texts.

> There is a universal tendency among mankind to conceive all beings like themselves, and to transfer to every object, those qualities, with which they are familiarly acquainted, and of which they are intimately conscious. We find human faces in the moon, armies in the clouds; and by a natural propensity, if not corrected by experience and reflection, ascribe malice or good-will to everything, that hurts or pleases us…
>
> David Hume, The Natural History of Religion

A writer might choose to anthropomorphise a god, an animal, object or even a setting—a setting that is in some way sentient and actively working against a protagonist can be seen in Gothic works such as Poe's *The Fall of the House of Usher* and Stoker's *Dracula*.

In his fantasy novel, Mervyn Peake uses anthropomorphism to capture the otherworldly nature of Gormenghast castle:

> This tower, patched unevenly with black ivy, arose like a mutilated finger from among the fists of knuckled masonry and pointed blasphemously at heaven. At night the owls made of it an echoing throat; by day it stood voiceless and cast its long shadow. Mervyn Peake, Gormenghast

A fine line exists between anthropomorphism and PERSONIFICATION (see page 28). Personification is a figurative device whereas anthropomorphism is to be taken literally. For example, these doors really do behave as stated:

> ... there were doors that wouldn't open unless you asked politely, or tickled them in exactly the right place ... J. K. Rowling, Harry Potter and the Philosopher's Stone

Rowling imbues parts of her setting with anthropomorphic traits to add to the sense of the enchanted and magical. Or take this extract from perhaps the most famous example of anthropomorphism in literature:

> The animals were all at work weeding turnips under the supervision of a pig, when they were astonished to see Benjamin come galloping from the direction of the farm buildings, braying at the top of his voice. It was the first time that they had ever seen Benjamin excited — indeed, it was the first time that anyone had ever seen him gallop. "Quick, quick!" he shouted. "Come at once! They're taking Boxer away!" Without waiting for orders from the pig, the animals broke off work and raced back to the farm buildings. Sure enough, there in the yard was a large closed van, drawn by two horses, with lettering on its side and a sly-looking man in a low-crowned bowler hat sitting on the driver's seat. And Boxer's stall was empty. George Orwell, Animal Farm

Writers should see themselves as playing with language; it is a creative tool to be enjoyed.

PERSONIFICATION
smiling stars and gloomy clouds

PERSONIFICATION (French *personne* 'represent or embody') is a popular device. Like anthropomorphism, it attributes human traits to non-human things, but only as part of a description to enhance an impression:

The flowers danced in the breeze. *The moon peeped through the clouds.*

Personification can take a simple noun and turn it into something with a degree of figurative agency, as well as reflecting character and attitude:

Busy old fool, unruly sun,
Why dost thou thus,
Through windows, and through curtains call on us? John Donne, The Sun Rising

This creates a mental image of the sun as an ancient and bumbling man and also captures the warm impudence of the author.

These are the lips of the lake, on which no beard grows. It licks its chops from time to time. Henry David Thoreau, Walden

The personification of the lake as a giant inverted mouth presents a new way of looking at the experience of standing by a lake. The present tense *these are...* and the colloquial register *chops* lead the reader in and put them at ease. The use of alliteration (*see page 52*) in *lips*, *lake* and *lick* emulates the lapping of the waves on the shore, creating a powerful image.

"I like everything about the car, except its expression."

ZOOMORPHISM
you angel

ZOOMORPHISM is the inverse of personification and anthromorphism—it is the attribution of animalistic traits to humans. Everyday English is full of playful zoomorphic phrases: *What a lamb; You're barking up the wrong tree; You shy little mouse; Spread your wings; He's a sly fox.* We use many zoomorphic insults: *Chicken! Bitch! Pig! Cow! Rat! Toad! Worm!* A 1912 letter by D. H. Lawrence following the rejection of his novel *Sons and Lovers* is full of wrathful zoomorphic descriptions of the English public:

> Curse the blasted, jelly-boned swines, the slimy, the belly-wriggling invertebrates, the miserable sodding rotters, the flaming sods, the snivelling, dribbling, dithering palsied pulse-less lot that make up England today. They've got white of egg in their veins, and their spunk is that watery it's a marvel they can breed. They can but frog-spawn — the gibberers! D. H. Lawrence, Letter to Edward Garnett

Zoomorphism is an excellent device for capturing character. In *Wuthering Heights*, Heathcliff is frequently described using animalistic imagery, as in Cathy's description below in which she unsuccessfully attempts to warn Isabella Linton of his predatory nature:

> 'Pray, don't imagine that he conceals depths of benevolence and affection beneath a stern exterior! He's not a rough diamond – a pearl-containing oyster of a rustic: he's a fierce, pitiless, wolfish man.' Emily Brontë, Wuthering Heights

METAPHOR
you're a diamond

A METAPHOR says that one thing *is* another thing, even though this is not literally true. A common figurative device with a long and rich history, it allows writers to make connections which appeal to their readers' wider experiences and help them see the subject in a fresh and original way:

Life is a journey.

That is music to my ears.

He has a heart of stone.

She's a thorn in my side.

Many simple metaphors can become *extended* into subsequent phrases where they can help frame complex and abstract ideas for readers:

Life is a banquet, and most poor suckers are starving to death! Patrick Dennis, Auntie Mame

All the world's a stage, and all the men and women merely players. They have their exits and their entrances. William Shakespeare, As You Like It

Art washes away from the soul the dust of everyday life. Pablo Picasso

If you want a love message to be heard, it has got to be sent out. To keep a lamp burning, we have to keep putting oil in it. Mother Teresa

Almost all writers and philosophers have examined metaphor:

But the greatest thing by far is to be a master of metaphor. It is the one thing that cannot be learnt from others; and it is also a sign of genius, since a good metaphor implies an intuitive perception. … There are three stances that poets have chosen: 1) to versify them in automatic ways. 2) to deploy them masterfully, combining them, extending them and crystallizing them in strong images. 3) to step outside the ordinary ways we think metaphorically and employ them in unusual ways. Aristotle Poetics (collage)

Metaphors are also useful for delivering juxtaposition (*see pages 22–23*):

> *Delia was an overbearing cake with condescending frosting, and frankly, I was on a diet.* Maggie Stiefvater, Lament: The Faerie Queen's Deception

> *The parents looked upon Matilda in particular as nothing more than a scab. A scab is something you have to put up with until the time comes when you can pick it off and flick it away.* Roald Dahl, Matilda

Metaphors can easily become clichéd or forced, jarring a reader out of a narrative, so read widely and soak up as many examples of convincing and (equally valuable) disappointing metaphors as you can.

Author Orson Scott Card says that *Metaphors have a way of holding the most truth in the least space* and Haruki Murakami, in *Kafka on the Shore*, writes that *metaphors can reduce the distance... metaphors help eliminate what separates you and me*. Many of the finest examples of prose and poetry rely on metaphor and reader interpretation to convey complex messages in as simple a form as possible. Using the figurative to create a shared image between the writer and the reader helps break down the boundaries that exist between them.

Some writers have argued that we live and develop through metaphorical interpretation of the world around us, including ourselves. In this vein, Goethe writes that *All that is transitory is but a metaphor*.

SIMILE & ANALOGY
like peas in a pod

A SIMILE draws a comparison between one thing and another, usually by using the words 'like' or 'as'. Similar to metaphors (*pp. 28–29*), similes expand and illustrate by giving an example. Many are used every day:

> He smokes like a chimney.   It was as dry as a bone.
>
> They fight like cats and dogs. She's bright as a button.

In literature, similes can contribute humour:

> Elderly American ladies leaning on their canes listed toward me like towers of Pisa.
>
> Vladimir Nabokov, Lolita

or highlight colour and texture (or the paucity of it, as here):

> She was a pale blonde with a skin like clean and polished bone. John Steinbeck, East of Eden

or auditory description, here the sound of giggling:

> Mr. Toots was sure to hail this with a burst of chuckles, like the opening of a bottle of some effervescent beverage. Charles Dickens, Dombey and Son

A simile can also be used to soften a potentially offensive comparison. Here, Dr Johnson compares writers Samuel Richardson and Henry Fielding:

> … there was as great a difference between them, as between a man who knew how a watch was made, and a man who could tell the hour by looking at the dial-plate. James Boswell, Life of Samuel Johnson

As with metaphor, a simile requires careful handling if a writer is to both maintain the integrity of an established tone and provide original and unique description:

As a rule, the comparison should be close enough to the poem's concerns to appear to the reader as natural enough to draw on its argumentative or thematic circuitry, and distant enough to arrest the reader within its felicity and originality, without breaking the spell of the poem. Don Paterson, The Empty Image

An EPIC or HOMERIC SIMILE unfolds over several lines, typically in the form like [or as] a _____ when it _____. In this example from Homer's *Illiad*, Hector awaits the approach of Achilles:

> As a snake in the hills, guarding his hole, awaits a man bloated with poison, deadly hatred seething inside him, glances flashing fire as he coils round his lair.

Milton's *Paradise Lost* is also full of Homeric similes. They complement epic poetry and spoken word as they expand important details and help build towards a climax (in prose, however, they can be distracting).

Metaphors and similes are both tools which draw an ANALOGY. However, an analogy can also be drawn without either:

> JULIET: What's in a name? that which we call a rose
>   By any other word would smell as sweet; William Shakespeare, Romeo and Juliet

Analogies can be extended into PARABLES, simple stories which teach simple lessons, and longer ALLEGORIES, stories where characters, events and settings may all function as symbols, ripe for interpretation by the reader.

"Candice, your eyes are like two crystal-blue pools of habitual judgment."

Synecdoche
nice wheels

SYNECDOCHE (pronounced *sin-**neck**-dough-key*) is a device where a part is used to refer to the whole. Here are some common examples:

<u>Wheels</u> — *slang for a car*

<u>Boots</u> *on the ground* — *soldiers in action*

ask for her <u>hand</u> — *asking to marry*

Room full of <u>suits</u> — *businessmen*

40-<u>head</u> — *count of cattle*

Fresh <u>blood</u> — *new members*

A synecdoche is a form of metaphor, but by choosing a part to stand for the whole a writer selects a figurative focal point for that whole's identity. For example *boots on the ground* emphasises the 'boot' (something used to tread down, to supress) as well as the 'ground' (territory being fought over).

In Charlie Kaufman's 2008 movie *Synecdoche, New York*, the story follows obsessive theatre director Caden Cotard as he becomes increasingly embroiled in his own creations. Set in the fictional town of Schenectady, the film presents itself as a synecdoche, a small part (the story) being used to represent the whole (American society).

Caden's huge, mad, pasteboard world stands for the real world, is part of it, is superimposed on to it, and finally melts into it.

Peter Bradshaw, Review in *The Guardian*

METONYMY
delicious dish

METONYMY is similar to synecdoche but instead of using a part to refer to a whole, a conceptually related object is used instead. For example:

The <u>Crown</u> — king or queen	<u>Hollywood</u> — US movie industry
Lend me a <u>hand</u> — help	Lend me your <u>ears</u> — listen
Go to <u>bed</u> — go to <u>sleep</u>	<u>England</u> beat <u>Spain</u> — football teams

Metonymy often represents industries or official bodies by the space they inhabit. Thus The Pentagon represents the US department of defence; The Kremlin represents the Russian government; The City represents the UK banking sector; Silicon Valley the US technology sector.

Some literary metonyms are so profound they become proverbs:

> The pen is mightier than the sword. Edward Bulwer-Lytton, *Richelieu*

This contains contains two metonyms: *pen* represents writing and writers, and *sword* stands in for physical power and soldiers.

Another common metonym in literature is the use of blood to represent life, as here which a young boy is injured at a saw mill:

> ... he swung toward them holding up the hand
> Half in appeal, but half as if to keep
> The life from spilling. Robert Frost, 'Out, Out—'

Metonymy can be used to create personification (*see page 28*) and add to the figurative nature of a description. For example *Rifles were guarding the gate* uses metonymy to give the weapons themselves a sense of agency, adding to the drama of the scene.

Motif
mirror mirror

A MOTIF is a recurring symbol in a literary work (e.g. light, as a symbol of hope). A TROPE (*page 38*) is the recurrence of a symbol across multiple works. Motifs are used to develop a particular THEME, character or idea.

The green light at the end of the pier in F. Scott Fitzgerald's *The Great Gatsby* is one of the most famous motifs in literature:

> *Involuntarily I glanced seaward — and distinguished nothing except a single green light, minute and far away, that might have been the end of a dock.* – Chapter 1

> *"If it wasn't for the mist we could see your home across the bay," said Gatsby. "You always have a green light that burns all night at the end of your dock."* – Chapter 5

> *It had seemed as close as a star to the moon. Now it was again a green light on a dock. His count of enchanted objects had diminished by one.* – Chapter 5

> *And as I sat there brooding on the old, unknown world, I thought of Gatsby's wonder when he first picked out the green light at the end of Daisy's dock* – Chapter 9

> *Gatsby believed in the green light, the orgiastic future that year by year recedes before us.* – Chapter 9

The green light represents the American Dream; its unobtainability across the social divide is one of the book's central themes. The motif is introduced in the first chapter, then recalled just over halfway through in chapter five (encouraging the reader to reflect on the progress of events since that time) and then returned to in the famous closing lines of the novel, emphasising the tragedy of lost hope.

In Joseph Conrad's *Heart of Darkness*, a motif of observation and eavesdropping plays against a second motif of contrast between exterior and interior spaces. Marlow, the protagonist, keenly observes his surroundings and listens to conversations. Initially, he does this superficially, but as he journeys more deeply into the heart of darkness, he gains deeper insights into his own and others' dark natures.

Motifs are powerful allegorical symbols which move a narrative along, encourage reflection and exemplify Show-Don't-Tell (*see page 4*). They also function as literary riddles, as the joy of unpicking them rewards readers with a richer illumination of the text:

> Those texts that appear to reward this reader for this additional investment - texts that we find exceptionally suggestive, apposite, or musical - are usually adjudged to be 'poetic'. ... The work of the poet is to contribute a text that will firstly invite such a reading; and secondly reward such a reading.   Don Paterson, The Poem

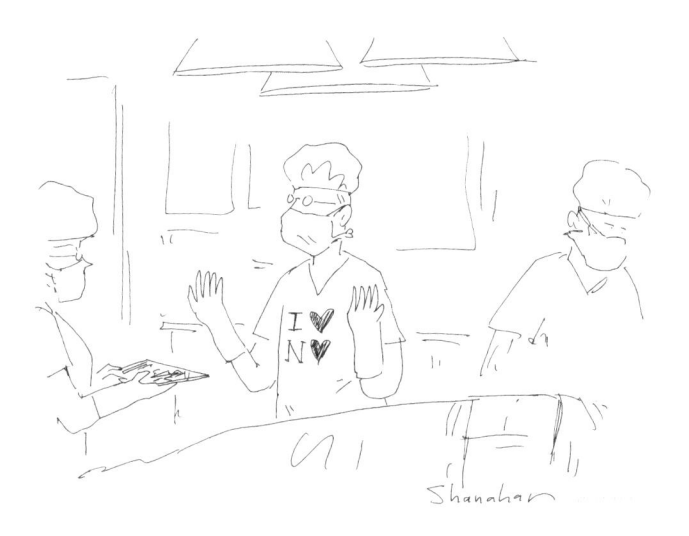

TROPE
a man goes into a bar

A TROPE (Greek *tropos*, to turn, change) once meant a twist in a plot. Today it also means any well-worn device, motif or theme which has become common across multiple works, even to the point of becoming a cliché:

ITEM TROPES include a *MacGuffin* (useless item everyone is after); *Flying Car*; *Wooden Stake*; *Unfired Guns*; *Cigarette in Ashtray*; *Big Hat*; *Umbrella* (*see page 4*). In the *The Cornetto Trilogy* (three comedic films directed by Edgar Wright: *Shaun of the Dead*, *Hot Fuzz* and *The World's End*), each film features a Cornetto ice cream in one or more scenes, creating a trope across the series. This is increasingly typical in screenwriting, as tropes, like motifs, involve rewarding interactions with the audience and are also used to develop style and brand.

CHARACTER TROPES include *Handsome Hero*; *Haunted Heroine*; *Amazing Dog*; *Almost-Human Robot*; *Creepy Housekeeper*; *Hired Gun*; *Punk Schoolgirl*; *Action Dad*; *Ladykiller in Love*; *Teenage Assassin*; *Unshaven Detective*; *Bromantic Foil*. A character trope for the typical hero is that they have self-assurance which at times can appear arrogant (something Aristotle refers to as *hubris*). From superheroes to the character of Hamlet, the hero struggles as a difficult but exceptional being in an unexceptional world:

The reasonable man adapts himself to the world: the unreasonable one persists in trying to adapt the world to himself. Therefore all progress depends on the unreasonable man.
George Bernard Shaw, The Revolutionist's Handbook

GENRE TROPES include *Everyone is a Suspect*; *Happily Ever After*; *Almost Kiss*; *He's Back*; *Break his Heart to Save Him*; *Alien Invasion*; *The Chase*; *Find the Cure*.

A genre trope in detective fiction is the 'big reveal' at the end, where all loose ends are tied together:

> "Is it possible? My poor friend! You have not yet realized that it was Miss Howard who went to the chemist's shop?"
>
> "Miss Howard?"
>
> "But, certainly. Who else?" Agatha Christie, The Mysterious Affair at Styles

NARRATIVE TROPES include Cut to Funeral; Polished Shoes on Desert Sand; Blow up the Set; Almost Out of Oxygen; Can't Tie His Tie; Emergency Broadcast; Soft Focus on Crush; Sarcastic Clapping; Unable to Cry; Gritty Colouring; etc. A typical example might be the line, *"Your mission, should you choose to accept it ..."*.

You get the idea—there are thousands. Note how in each example above, a few words suffice to conjure entire scenes. Tropes go in and out of fashion—Romantic writers used tropes of blue flowers and nightingales.

"You ever wonder why they always only draw one tree?"

ADNOMINATION
once a pun a paranomasia

Many words can be broken into *morphemes*. For example, the word **unfounded** is formed of three morphemes, **un** (a prefix we use to mean not), **found** (the root morpheme that the word is built around) and **ed** (a suffix used to denote the past tense). ADNOMINATION is the repetition of a morpheme across different words. Take the company motto of Harrods of London:

Everything for Everybody Everywhere.

This example repeats the morpheme *every* three times. Or take the lyrics from Tom Petty's *Refugee*, where the root morpheme *some* is repeated four times in different constructions:

Somewhere, somehow, somebody must have kicked you around some.

Adnomination is closely related to ANAPHORA and EPIPHORA (*see pages 18–19*) as it builds emphasis. In poetry, songwriting and prose, such devices can add a sense of metre and rhythm as well as of verbal play.

A special form of adnomination is PARONOMASIA, better known as PUNNING, when two words sound the same but have different meanings or spellings. This device is most often used for its comedic effect:

Atheism is a non-prophet organization. George Carlin

William Shakespeare employed more than 3000 puns in his plays:

Ask for me to-morrow, and you shall find me a grave man. Mercutio, in *Romeo and Juliet*

Mercutio, fatally stabbed, still manages to jest with Romeo and Benvolio. Paronomasia can also be wielded to demonstrate confusion:

"Mine is a long and a sad tale!" said the Mouse, turning to Alice, and sighing.
"It is a long tail, certainly," said Alice, looking down with wonder at the Mouse's
tail; "but why do you call it sad?" Lewis Carroll, *Alice's Adventures in Wonderland*

COMPOUND PUNS, containing two or more puns, are a great staple of comedy writing, as in this example, attributed to Richard Whately:

Q. Why can a man never starve in the Great Desert?
A. Because he can eat the sand which is there.
Q: But what brought the sandwiches there?
A: Why, Noah sent Ham, and his descendants mustered and bred.

These smart devices can also help present complex ideas in more playful ways, as in this declaration by Socrates, from Plato's *Apology*:

I am wiser than this man, for neither of us appears to know anything great and good; but he fancies he knows something, although he knows nothing; whereas I, as I do not know anything, so I do not fancy I do. In this trifling particular, then, I appear to be wiser than he, because I do not fancy I know what I do not know.

"Let's faunicate."

ANASTROPHE
& antimetabole & chiasmus

ANASTROPHE inverts the common word order in a sentence, e.g. by:

- ★ Placing an adjective after the noun it modifies: *the woman wise*.
- ★ Placing a verb before its noun: *screamed the crowd*.
- ★ Placing a noun before its preposition: *worlds between*.

Take the opening lines of Coleridge's *Kubla Khan*:

> In Xanadu <u>did</u> Kubla Khan | A stately pleasure-dome <u>decree</u>:
> Where Alph, the sacred river, ran | Through <u>caverns</u> measureless to man
> Down to a sunless sea. Samuel Taylor Coleridge, *Kubla Khan*

Coleridge's use of anastrophe here adds an archaic element to the language, giving it a timeless, dreamlike quality.

In modern English, premodifying adjectives come in a specific order, usually learnt subconsciously at a young age. For example, we tend to say *The large black dog*, rather than *The black large dog*. Here is that hidden order:

1.	OPINION	*clever, cruel, beautiful*
2.	SIZE	*large, small, short*
3.	PHYSICAL QUALITY	*soft, rough, transparent*
4.	SHAPE	*round, hollow, square*
5.	AGE	*young, ancient, teenage*
6.	COLOUR	*purple, red, green*
7.	ORIGIN	*British, Japanese, Ghanaian*
8.	MATERIAL	*porcelain, wood, plastic*
9.	TYPE	*general-purpose, four-sided, U-shaped*
10.	PURPOSE	*cleaning, hammering, cooking*

> *I first tried to write a story when I was about seven. It was about a dragon. I remember nothing about it except a philological fact. My mother said nothing about the dragon, but pointed out that one could not say 'a green great dragon', but had to say 'a great green dragon'. I wondered why, and still do.* J. R. R. Tolkien *Letters*

Inverting the standard adjective order is a further form of anastrophe which can draw attention to a key element of description:

> *… she smiled often. A slow widening of her thin black lips to show even, small white teeth, then the slow effortless closing.* Maya Angelou, *I Know Why the Caged Birds Sings*

Here Angelou has fronted the adjective 'even' to emphasise the fascinatingly unnatural perfection of the smile.

Another figurative device involving changing word order is is CHIASMUS:

> **By day the frolic, and the dance by night.** Samuel Johnson, *The Vanity of Human Wishes*

> **Despised, if ugly; if she's fair, betrayed.** Mary Leapor, *An Essay on Woman*

Chiasmus uses two pairs of words, one contrasting and one similar in meaning (day/night, frolic/dance and *despised/betrayed, ugly/fair*), the ordering being reversed in the second instance. Chiasmic phrases are best used sparingly to convey a particularly poignant or striking description or idea.

A repeated word within a chiasmus turns it into an ANTIMETABOLE:

> **And so, my fellow Americans: ask not what your country can do for you—ask what you can do for your country.** John F. Kennedy, *Inaugural Address*

> **Fair is foul and foul is fair.** William Shakespeare, *Macbeth*

> **With my mind on my money and my money on my mind.** Snoop Dog, *Gin and Juice*

Antimetabole can be used for persuasion, for atmospheric description and for verbal play.

KENNING
& portmanteau

KENNING (Old Norse, *kenna* 'know, perceive') is an ancient device that describes a familiar noun in an unfamiliar, metaphorical way. It has its origin in Scandinavian and Old English oral poetry. Northrop Frye in his *Anatomy of Criticism* refers to a kenning as being like a spell, an oracle or a riddle *more primitive than a presentation of subjective feelings*. Here are some examples, most from the Old English poem *Beowulf*:

OLD ENGLISH	ENGLISH	MEANING
bánhús	bone house	body
hronráde	whale road	sea
hildeswát	battle sweat	blood
hildeléoman	light of battle	sword
grennir gunn-másfeeder of ravens		warrior

In the following line from an Icelandic saga, when absent Gunnlaug's lovely bride-to-be Helga is married off to Hfran, Gunnlaug declares:

> **In two I'll slice the hair-seat / of Helga's kiss-gulper.** 13th C. *Saga of Gunnlaug Serpent-Tongue*

Hair-seat here means 'head', and Hfran is seen as having stolen Helga's kisses—hence, he is a kiss-gulper. So Gunnlaug is swearing to cleave the head of Helga's new husband Hfran.

In his 1939 novel, *Finnegans Wake*, James Joyce regularly deploys kenning (*and portmanteau, see facing page*) alongside references to Nordic culture:

> And aweigh he yankered on the Norgean run so that seven sailend sonnenrounders was he breastbare to the brina-bath, where bottoms out has fatthoms full, fram Franz Josè Land til Cabo Thormendoso, evenstarde and risingsoon.

(And he weighed anchor on the Norwegian run sailing silently on the fathomless sea for seven years, from Franz Jose to Cabo Thormendoso, from the evening star to the rising sun).

PORTMANTEAU has a similar quality to kenning and is a term originally coined by Lewis Carroll to describe a hybrid word blended from two others, as demonstrated here in his poem *Jabberwocky*:

> *'Twas brillig, and the slithy toves | Did gyre and gimble in the wabe:*
> *All mimsy were the borogoves, | And the mome raths outgrabe.*

Caroll later uses Humpty Dumpty to explain *slithy* to Alice:

> "Well, 'slithy' means 'lithe and slimy'. 'Lithe' is the same as 'active'. You see it's like a portmanteau — there are two meanings packed up into one word."
>
> Lewis Caroll, Through the Looking-Glass

Common modern examples are *smog* (smoke + fog), *snarky* (snide + remark), *bromance*, *brunch*, *romcom*, *glamping*, the bodice-ripping *bodacious* (bold + audacious), *moped* (motor + pedal) and *fortnight* (fourteen + nights).

"Another Martoonie?"

Paradox & Bathos
& paraprodokian

A PARADOX is a statement that contradicts itself but also contains a grain of truth: *Less is more; You have to be cruel to be kind; I am nobody.* A paradoxical statement can be used to show a shallowness of character:

> SIR ROBERT CHILTERN: *You prefer to be natural?*
> MRS. CHEVELEY: *Sometimes. But it is such a very difficult pose to keep up.*
>
> Oscar Wilde, An Ideal Husband

or to create a sense of irony in a consciously contradictory statement:

> *All animals are equal but some are more equal than others.* Geroge Orwell, Animal Farm

or for pure delight of language:

> DARLINGTON: *I can resist everything except temptation.* Oscar Wilde, Lady Windemere's Fan

BATHOS is a literary term introduced by Alexander Pope in 1727. It describes the effect of a writer treating a subject that is some way elevated or emotional with over-the-top language, therefore rendering it ridiculous.

Although originally a derogatory term for over-pompous writing, modern writers have embraced bathos, and it is now regularly employed in literature, film and television to create comedy through anticlimax. Bathos can change a moment of profundity into one of hilarity, a self-conscious bubble-bursting which helps avoid taking things too seriously:

> "You know," said Arthur, "it's at times like this, when I'm trapped in a Vogon airlock with a man from Betelgeuse, and about to die of asphyxiation in deep space that I really wish I'd listened to what my mother told me when I was young."
> "Why, what did she tell you?"
> "I don't know, I didn't listen." Douglas Adams, *The Hitchhiker's Guide to the Galaxy*

Absurdist playwright Samuel Beckett also frequently applies bathos:

> HAMM: Why don't you kill me?
> CLOV: I don't know the combination of the cupboard. Samuel Beckett, *Endgame*

PARAPROSDOKIAN is another popular comedy device. Paraprosdokians are two-part statements. The first part builds the suggestion of a common cliché. However, in the second part, that expectation is overturned with a sudden slapstick twist, creating a bathetic anticlimax:

> I've had a perfectly wonderful evening, but this wasn't it. Groucho Marx

> War does not determine who is right — only who is left. Bertrand Russell

> If all the girls who attended the Yale prom were laid from end to end, I wouldn't be at all surprised. Dorothy Parker, *While Rome Burns*

> The cook was a good cook, as cooks go; and as cooks go she went. Saki, *Reginald*

TMESIS
& spoonerism

TMESIS (Greek *tmesis* 'cutting') is the insertion of a word into another word, the insertion coming before the main stressed syllable. In Australian English, it is referred to as *tumbarumba*. In the 1964 movie *My Fair Lady*, lyricist Alan Jay Lerner employs tmesis in Eliza Dolittle's speech to project her untidy mind and uneducated lower class Cockney background:

'fan-bloody-tastic'   'abso-blooming-lutley'.

Tmesis is common in spoken language, e.g. in *That's a whole nother story* the word *whole* has been inserted into *another*, and in *Romeo and Juliet*, lovestruck Romeo dreamily speaks of himself in the third person and uses tmesis:

This is not Romeo, he's some other where. William Shakespeare, *Romeo and Juliet*

Most tmesis, however, involves the insertion of swear words, as above, or e.g.: *super-bloody-natural*, *cata-fucking-strophic* and *ri-shitting-diculous*.

SPOONERISMS involve swapping the beginnings of two words, their first letters or first morphemes. So for example *touch down* becomes *dutch town* and *mind-blowing* becomes *blind-mowing*. They are named after the Reverend William Archibald Spooner, who regularly came out with things like:

It is kisstomary to cuss the bride.   What a blushing crow.
You have tasted a whole worm.   That's a well-boiled icicle.

Enormous fun can be had with this device, and many jokes rely on it:

Q: What's the difference between a a dirty bus stop and a lobster in a bra?
A: One's a crusty bus station and the other's a busty crustacean.

ZEUGMA
fishing for fish and for fun

ZEUGMA (Greek *zeugma* 'yoking; a bond, a band') is another form of often comedic verbal game, although quite subtle. Zeugma is when a modifier in a sentence, usually an adjective or a verb, is applied to two (or more) nouns, usually one mundane and one more abstract. For example: He was hungry for pizza and for love or She broke his car and his heart.

Mark Twain uses zeugma in *The Adventures of Tom Sawyer* to describe his protagonist's altercation with the 'new boy' in his neighbourhood:

> [They] covered themselves with dust and glory.

Here, zeugma paints a quiet, everyday sadness over a dinner scene:

> We were partners, not soul mates,
> two separate people who happened
> to be sharing a menu and a life.
>
> Amy Tan, The Hundred Secret Senses

Zeugma can also be found in newspaper headlines to entertain and inform, as in the two examples below from the *New York Times*:

> Murray Loses Cool and, Soon, the Match

> An Afghan Poet Shapes Metal and Hard Words

CACOPHONY
& euphony & onomatopoeia

CACOPHONY (Greek *kakophonos* 'harsh sounding'), or dissonance, is the deliberate use of jarring or unpleasant plosive, sibilant and fricative sounds (*see page 11*) to create a discordant piece that is challenging to read:

> Out, damned spot! Out, I say! —
> One: two: why, then, 'tis time to do't. William Shakespeare, *Macbeth*

Shakespeare uses cacophony to indicate Lady Macbeth's madness. Or:

> ...all the war-propaganda, all the screaming and lies and hatred, comes invariably from people who are not fighting. George Orwell, *Homage to Catalonia*

Sylvia Plath's poem *The Colossus* begins with a cacophonous opening:

> I shall never get you put together entirely,
> Pieced, glued, and properly jointed.
> Mule-bray, pig-grunt and bawdy cackles
> Proceed from your great lips. Sylvia Plath, *The Colossus*

Note the frequency of plosive *t*, *p* and *d* sounds, harsh *ck* sounds, and zoomorphism (*see page 29*). Even the laterals sound sarcastic and biting.

EUPHONY (Greek *euphonia* 'sweetness of voice'), the opposite of cacophony, is the use of pleasant sounds, such as soft consonants and long vowels, as wells as rhythm, assonance and alliteration, to create a positive tone:

> Season of mists and mellow fruitfulness John Keats, *Ode to Autumn* (first line)

Keats uses sibilants, gentle rolling *m* and *n* nasals, *l* laterals and long vowel sounds s<u>ea</u>son, mell<u>ow</u>, along with alliteration <u>m</u>ists/<u>m</u>ellow and poetic metre to create a beautiful euphonic opening of an Autumn morning. Or:

> Shall I compare thee to a summer's day? William Shakespeare, Sonnet 18 (first line)

Euphony is also used in the world of advertising:

> Certainly, euphony should be a consideration in choosing a brand name. Lamolay sounds better than Tarytak for a toilet paper even though it has the same number of letters. John O'Shaughnessy, Consumer Behaviour: Perspectives, Findings and Explanations

ONOMATOPOEIA (Greek, 'word- or name-making') occurs when a word's sound matches the thing it describes. Examples are words like *bang, crash, clatter, click, hiss, fizz, buzz, gulp, gush, honk, plop, rip, roar, rustle, sizzle, sniff, smash, slap, slurp, splash, trickle, thump, thud, whizz, zip, zoom*. Onomatopoeia can make a text more three-dimensional to a reader by appealing to the sense of sound as well as sight in descriptions. Here, it adds tension to a ghost story:

> The only sounds I could hear above the trotting of the pony's hooves, the rumble of the wheels and the creak of the cart, were sudden, harsh, weird cries from birds near and far ... At first the pony and then the trap met the sandy path, the smart noise we had been making ceased, and we went on almost in silence save for a hissing, silky sort of sound. Here and there were clumps of reeds, bleached bone-pale, and now and again the faintest of winds caused them to rattle dryly. Susan Hill, The Woman in Black

Children's writers also frequently use onomatopoeia:

> Chug, chug, chug. Puff, puff, puff. Ding-dong, ding-dong.
> The little train rumbled over the tracks. Watty Piper, The Little Engine That Could

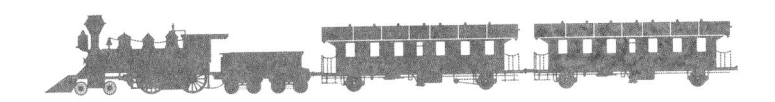

ALLITERATION & ASSONANCE
& consonance

ALLITERATION is the repetition of *initial or stressed consonant* sounds in words:

> Larry's lizard likes lounging aloft the lake.
>
> Chuck the chicken chewed a cherry.
>
> Seven singing sisters were assigned to Spain.
>
> Big bubbles above and below.
>
> Tim took twenty toys to tiny tots.
>
> Kim's kid kept kicking like crazy.

Note how, in the above examples, twenty, Spain and crazy only partially alliterate. Like so many literary devices, this one can be overused:

> Ages ago, Alex, Allen and Alva arrived at Antibes, and Alva allowing all, allowing anyone, against Alex's admonition, against Allen's angry assertion: another African amusement... anyhow, as all argued, an awesome African army assembled and arduously advanced against an African anthill, assiduously annihilating ant after ant, and afterward, Alex astonishingly accuses Albert as also accepting Africa's antipodal ant annexation. Walter Abish, *Alphabetical Africa*

Here are Vladimir Nabokov's opening lines to his most famous work:

> Lolita, light of my life, fire of my loins. My sin, my soul. Lo-lee-ta: the tip of the tongue taking a trip of three steps down the palate to tap, at three, on the teeth. Lo. Lee. Ta. Vladimir Nabokov, *Lolita*

Nabokov is encouraging us to play with the words in our mouths. It is almost irresistible to read this sentence and not say 'Lolita' aloud.

ASSONANCE is the repetition of *vowel* sounds:

> Try as I might, the kite would not fly.
>
> Kneel and feel the need for speed.
>
> Go slow over the road.
>
> Deaf men sell wedding bells.

Like alliteration, assonance is common in poetry and prose, and widely used in advertising (e.g Zanussi's *The Appliance of Science*). Dylan Thomas' famous villanelle, below, uses assonance through two vowel sounds, *a* (as in d*ay*) and *i* (as in n*ight*) to add internal rhyme and increase the pace of the poem, essential in this impassioned plea from a son to his dying father:

> Do not go gentle into that good night,
> Old age should burn and rave at close of day;
> Rage, rage, against the dying of the light.   Dylan Thomas, Do Not Go Gentle into that Good Night

CONSONANCE is the repetition of the *closing consonant* sounds of words:

With trucks, he takes rocks and bricks.	Scatter that litter, Potter.
Her foot left a wet print on the carpet.	Pen on chin, Len ran on in.
Impelling, compiling, bowling while smiling.	Don't trounce — dance once.

Much used in poetry, it is a weak form of end rhyme. Here, Wilfred Owen combines alliteration and consonance to give a visceral description:

> Let the boy try along this bayonet blade
> How cold steel is, and keen with hunger of blood;
> Blue with all malice, like a madman's flash;
> And thinly drawn with famishing for flesh.   Wilfred Owen, Arms and the Boy

Malapropism & Mondegreen
a comedy of errors

MALAPROPISM (French *mal à propos* 'inappropriately') involves replacing a word with another that sounds similar. This error of speech is normally given to foolish or vain characters, who use overly-complicated words they do not understand. The term originates from Richard Brinsley Sheridan's 1775 play, *The Rivals*, which features a self-important character called Mrs Malaprop who frequently muddles her words:

> *Promise to forget this fellow – to <u>illiterate</u> him, I say, quite from your memory.* [obliterate]
>
> *He is the very <u>pine-apple</u> of politeness!* [pinnacle]
>
> *I have since laid Sir Anthony's <u>preposition</u> before her.* [proposition]
>
> *I hope you will represent her to the captain as an object not altogether <u>illegible</u>.* [ineligible]
>
> *She might <u>reprehend</u> the true meaning of what she is saying.* [comprehend]

There are, however, even earlier uses of this comedic technique. Here is constable Dogberry from Shakespeare's *Much Ado About Nothing*:

> *Our watch, sir, have indeed <u>comprehended</u> two <u>auspicious</u> persons, and we would have them this morning examined before your worship.* [apprehended and suspicious]
>
> *O villain! Thou wilt be condemned into everlasting <u>redemption</u> for this.* [damnation]

Modern comedy writers also use the device. Here is Steve Carrell's character Michael Scott from the US series of *The Office*:

> *It was for charity. And I consider myself a great <u>philanderer</u>.* [philanthropist]
>
> *They are in for a bitter surprise. I am not one to be <u>truffled</u> with.* [trifled]
>
> *It wasn't me. They're trying to make me an <u>escape</u> goat.* [scape]

MONDEGREEN is a term coined in 1954 by American writer Sylvia Wright, whose mother used to read her this poem:

> Ye Highlands and ye Lowlands,
> Oh, where hae ye been?
> They hae slain the Earl o' Moray,
> And Lady Mondegreen. The Bonnie Earl o' Moray. Child Ballad No.181

The *actual* fourth line is And laid him on the green, which is homophonous. So, whilst a malapropism is a *misspeaking*, mondegreen is a *mishearing*.

Mondegreens commonly appear around song lyrics. For example, both There's a bathroom on the right [There's a bad moon on the rise, from *Bad Moon Rising* by Creedence Clearwater Revival] and 'Scuse me while I kiss this guy ['Scuse me while I kiss the sky from *Purple Haze* by Jimi Hendrix] became so well-known that the artists were actually known to sing the mondegreen form in live concerts. Sometimes a mondegreen can even replace the original, as in the *The Twelve Days of Christmas*, where nowadays we refer to four *calling* birds, a mondegreen of the original four *colly* [black] birds.

TAUTOLOGY & REDUPLICATION
wrong but not wrong wrong

TAUTOLOGY (Greek *tautologos* 'repeating what has been said') is the use of words that are synonymous, and so arguably superfluous, in a sentence:

> Smoking can kill you, and if you've been killed, you've lost a very important part of your life. Brooke Shields

> If we do not succeed, we run the risk of failure. Dan Quayle

> It's like déjà vu all over again. Yogi Berra

Not *succeeding* already implies failure and *déjà vu* already means *seeing it again*—there is no need to say it twice. Writers are generally advised to avoid tautology; phrases such as *old antique, dry desert, frozen ice, evening sunset, short summary, necessary requirement, sad misfortune, top summit, new innovation,* or *close proximity* tend to jar with readers. But used sparingly and deliberately tautology can be used for comedic effect and to develop character:

> I shall slip unnoticed through the darkness... like a dark, unnoticeable slippy thing.

This quote, from the film of Neil Gaiman's *Mirrormask*, shows a faintly ridiculous character trying to sound like an epic hero but becoming deflated, creating bathos (*see page 47*) through tautology. There is a similar quality to this next passage, in which Pooh proudly imagines a sign proclaiming:

North Pole — Discovered by Pooh — Pooh found it A. A. Milne, *Winnie-The-Pooh*

Advertisers employ tautology to draw attention to key themes:

Win a 100% Free Gift! With an Extra Added Bonus!

A *gift* is by its nature *free*, and a *bonus* is by definition *added*, however, the added emphasis makes the offer sound more appealing.

Sometimes a word is repeated twice to add extra level of meaning. This is an increasingly common device, known as REDUPLICATION:

"I like Chloe." "You mean you <u>like</u> like her?"

"Wow, it's hot today!" "Yes, but it's not <u>hot</u> hot."

"Want Soya milk?" "No, <u>milk</u> milk, please!"

"You talked to Craig?" "We didn't <u>talk</u> talk."

ORWELL'S 6 RULES FOR WRITERS

In his *Politics and the English Language*, George Orwell offers writers six rules for most writing:

1. Never use a metaphor, simile or other figure of speech which you are used to seeing in print.
2. Never use a long word where a short one will do.
3. If it is possible to cut a word out, always cut it out.
4. Never use the passive where you can use the active.
5. Never use a foreign phrase, a scientific word, or a jargon word if you can think of an everyday English equivalent.
6. Break any of these rules sooner than say anything outright barbarous.

VONNEGUT'S 8 RULES FOR WRITING

In *Bagombo Snuff Box: Uncollected Short Fiction*, Kurt Vonnegut offers eight rules for fiction:

1. Use the time of a total stranger in such a way that he or she will not feel the time was wasted.
2. Give the reader at least one character he or she can root for.
3. Every character should want something, even if it is only a glass of water.
4. Every sentence must do one of two things—reveal character or advance action.
5. Start as close to the end as possible.
6. Be a sadist. No matter how sweet and innocent your leading characters, make awful things happen to them – in order that the reader may see what they are made of.
7. Write to please just one person. If you open a window and make love to the world, so to speak, your story will get pneumonia.
8. Give your readers as much information as possible as soon as possible. To heck with suspense. Readers should have such complete understanding of what is going on, where and why, that they could finish the story themselves, should cockroaches eat the last few pages.